NO GOOD DOGS

by Peter Desberg

Illustrated by Betsy Rodden

A WALLABY BOOK
Published by SIMON & SCHUSTER
New York

WALLABY and colophon are registered trademarks of Simon & Schuster

First Wallaby Books printing November 1982

10 9 8 7 6 5 4 3 2 1

Manufactured in the United States of America

ISBN: 0-671-46081-1

CONTENTS

RESPONDING TO COMMANDS

The "Stay" command.

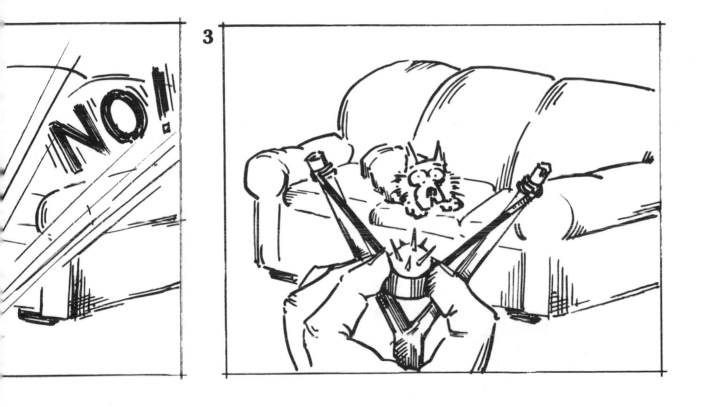

The "Catch" command.

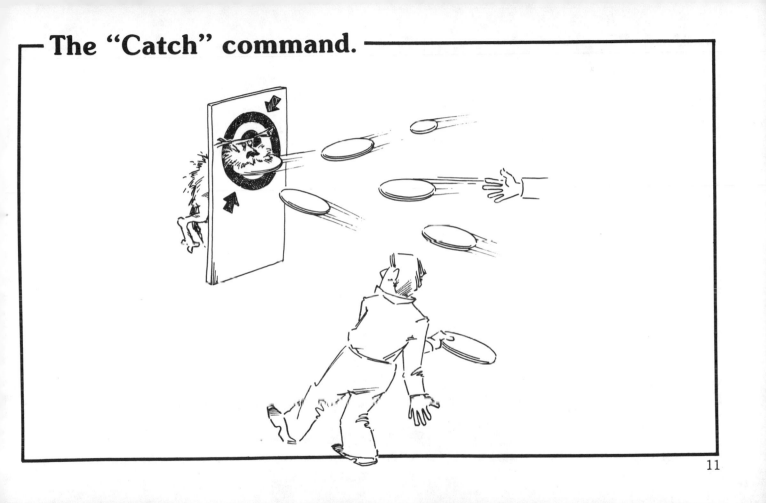

The "Heel" command: I.

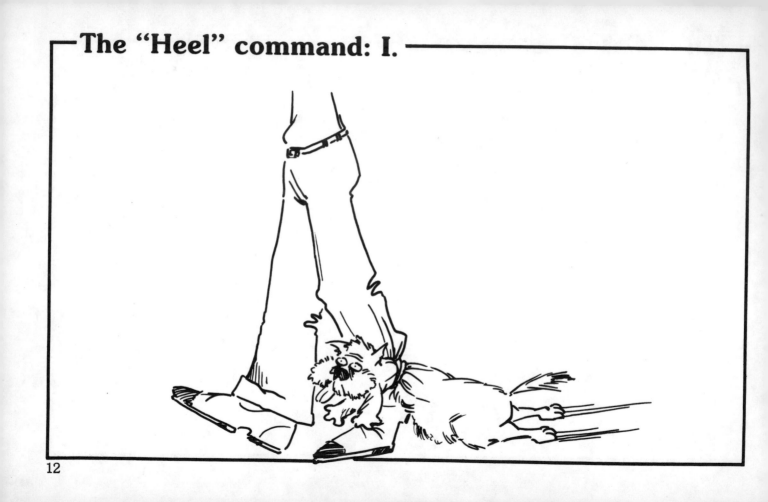

The "Heel" command: II
(for smaller dogs).

NOTE: This method of heel
training may lead to difficulties
with male dogs. If this problem
arises, see page 45.

The "Come!" command.

**Strong
Oppositional
Tendencies**

Stubborn

Independent

Obedient

Step 1: Call
Step 2: Pull

NOTE: To the left of the building is a Dog Personality Index which can be used to determine the appropriate training height.

The "Roll-over-and-play-dead" command.

— The "Sit" command.

1 Say the command "Sit" firmly.

2 Drop a heavy weight on the rear end.

3 In many cases, the dog's front paws will become tired if commanded to sit for long periods of time.

4 When front paws tire, they may receive outside support.

To make your dog responsive to his name, here are some suggestions for naming your dog.

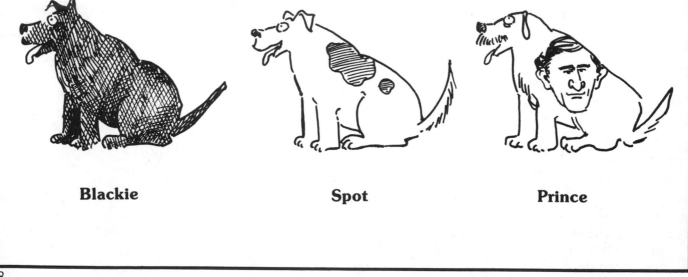

Blackie   Spot   Prince

TRAINING
FOR
GOOD HABITS

Paper training.

Getting accustomed to the postman.

Getting accustomed to the leash.

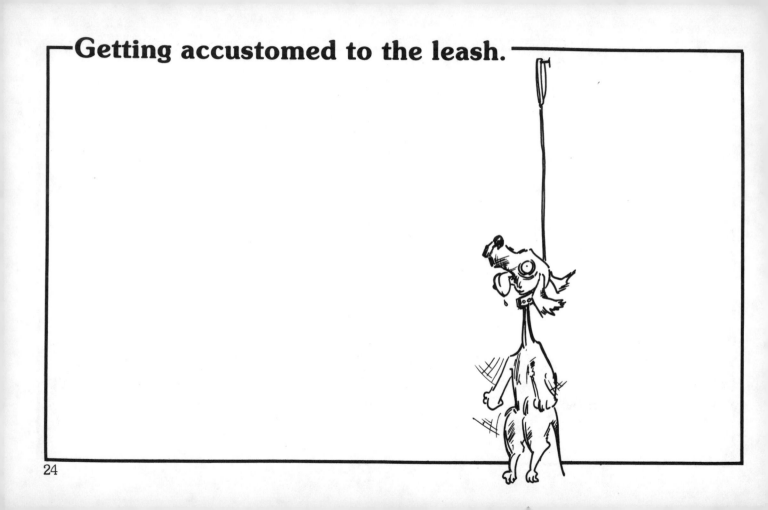

Bark at intruders: I.

Housebreaking.

Training the dog to appreciate dry dog food.

Getting the dog to exercise.

Fetching the newspaper.

1 Show dog the location of the paper.

2 Insert paper firmly in dog's mouth.

3 Kick dog to front door.

4 Remove paper.

5 Pat dog and praise.

1

2

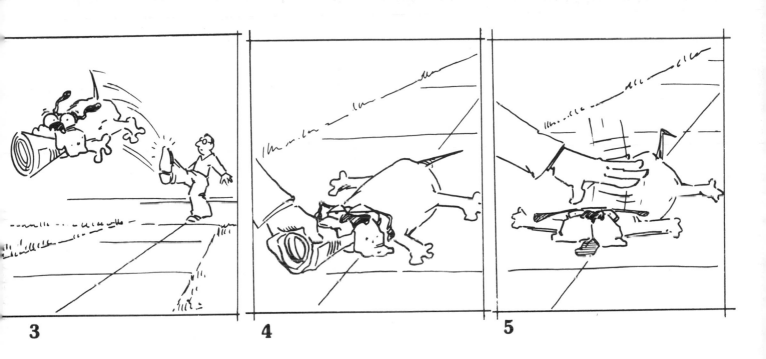

3

4

5

Learning to play with children.

Getting the dog accustomed to travel.

TRAINING FOR GOOD GROOMING

Getting rid of fleas and ticks.

Trouble-free bathing.

Keeping the dog clean.

NOTE: This device also helps keep the dog from soiling the carpets, maintains normal body temperature, and comes in four decorator colors. Dog owners will also find it a lot easier to wash this "doggie bag" than to wash the dog.

ELIMINATING BAD HABITS

Eliminate drooling.

Eliminate loud barking.

"HIS OWN VOICE"

Eliminate mounting people's legs when the male is feeling sensual.

Eliminate begging for scraps at the dinner table.

Eliminate jumping on guests' laps.

Eliminate chasing cats: II.

Eliminate scratching.

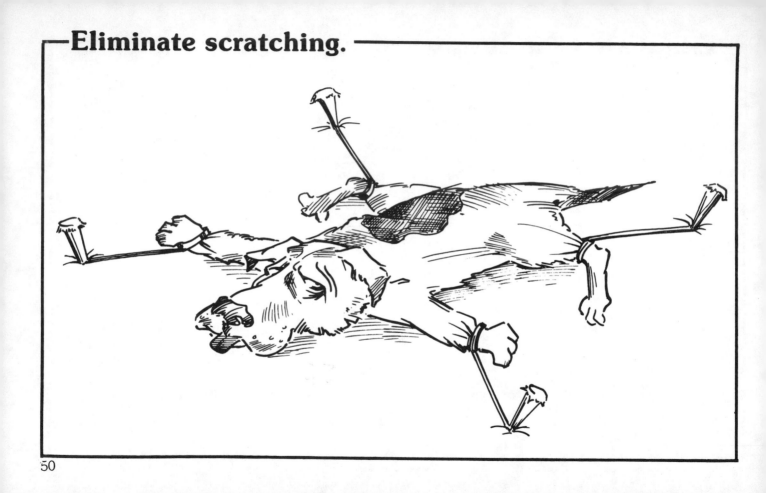

Eliminate sniffing other dogs' behinds.

Eliminate bringing home dead animals.

Step 1: Tie animal around dog's neck.

Step 2: Remove after three months.

Eliminate chewing on lamp cords.

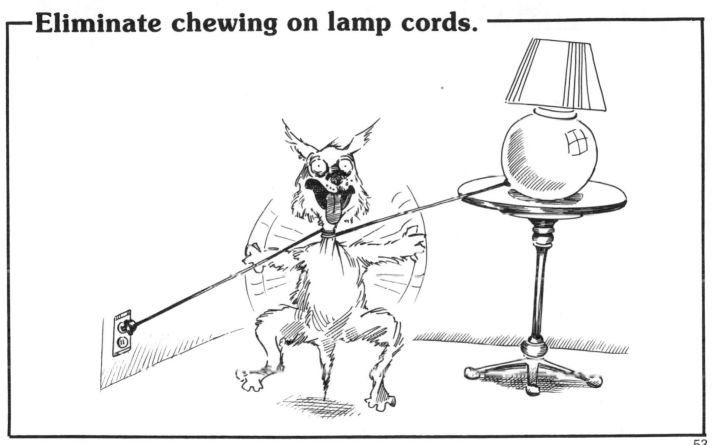

Eliminate shedding.

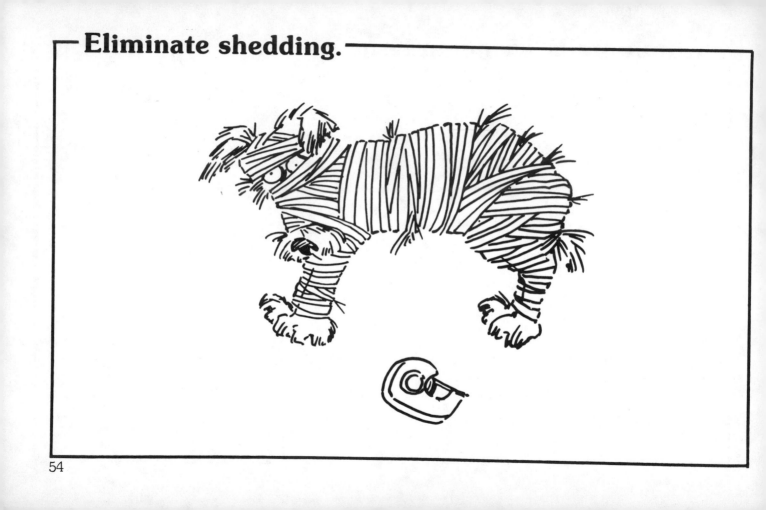

Eliminate licking people.

Eliminate smoking
in the adolescent dog.

Eliminate awakening the family in the early morning.

Eliminate chasing cars: I.

Eliminate chasing cars: II.

Eliminate "going" on the rug.

NOTE: Be sure to place the dog's nose as close to the point of violation (indicated above by the cross) as possible. Traditional dog trainers advise hitting the dog with a rolled-up newspaper. This is discouraged here because it would only bring a welcome distraction.

Eliminate neighborhood wandering by the bitch in heat.

Eliminate biting people's ankles.

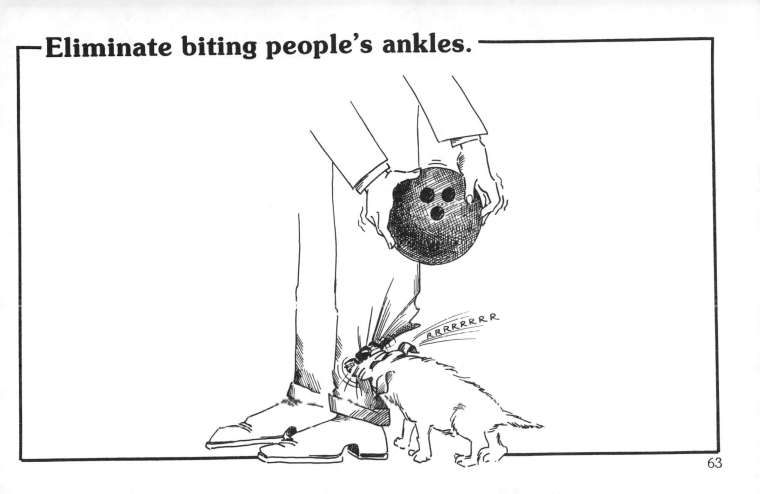

Eliminate chasing bicycles.

Eliminate chewing on furniture legs.

Eliminate poking around in the trash.

Eliminate sniffing people's crotches.

JOKES TO DEVELOP YOUR DOG'S SENSE OF HUMOR

You can't teach an old dog New Jersey.

Get a long little doggy.

A new dog pound.

His Bach is worse than his bite . . .

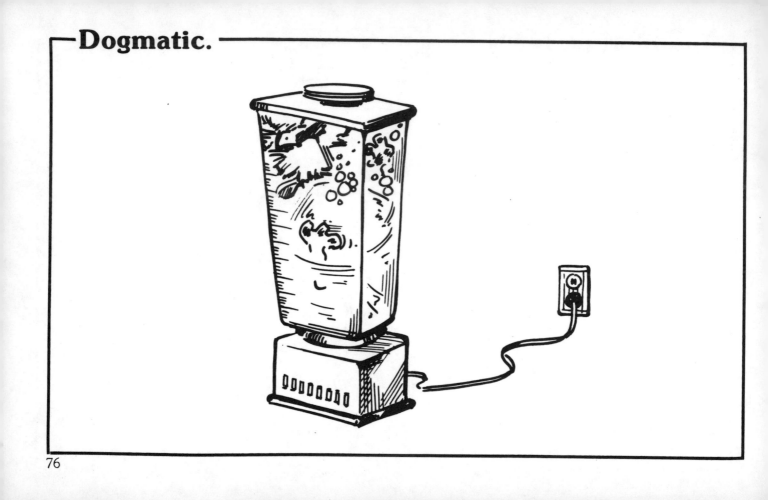

The bilingual dog.

Heavy petting.

Petting below the waist.

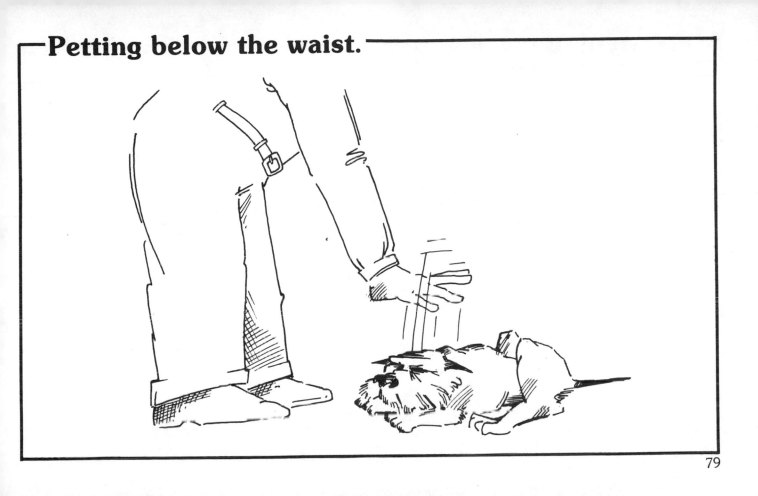

The canine mutiny.